FiESTA!

EGYPT

GROLIER
EDUCATIONAL

Published 1999 by Grolier Educational
Sherman Turnpike, Danbury, Connecticut.
Copyright © 1999 Times Editions Pte Ltd. Singapore.

Set ISBN: 0-7172-9324-6
Volume ISBN: 0-7172-9328-9

CIP information available from the Library of Congress or the publisher

Brown Partworks Ltd.

Series Editor: Tessa Paul
Series Designer: Joyce Mason
Crafts devised and created by Susan Moxley
Music arrangements by Harry Boteler
Photographs by Bruce Mackie
Production: Alex Mackenzie
Stylists: Joyce Mason and Tessa Paul

For this volume:
Writer: Christine Rodenbeck
Consultant: Mr. Mohammed Hanafee, Egyptian Consulate, London.
Editorial Assistants: Hannah Beardon and Paul Thompson

Printed in Italy

Adult supervision advised for all crafts and recipes,
particularly those involving sharp instruments and heat.

CONTENTS

EGYPT:

Egypt borders the Mediterranean Sea, but to the west and south are the Libyan and Nubian deserts. The Nile River, running through the country's center, creates a fertile strip in this wilderness of desert sands.

▶**The pyramids of Egypt** are among the great sights of the world. They were built by the Ancient Egyptians as tombs for their *pharaohs,* or kings. Nobody is certain how these massive stone structures were built.

Libya

First Impressions

- **Population** 58,236,000
- **Largest city** Cairo with a population of 11,642,000
- **Longest river** Nile
- **Highest mountain** Mt. Catherine at 8,668 ft.
- **Exports** Crude petroleum, cotton lint, textiles, fruit, and vegetables
- **Capital city** Cairo
- **Political status** Republic
- **Climate** Desert. Annual flooding of the Nile makes land fertile.
- **Art and culture** Site of ancient Egyptian buildings. Birthplace of the singer Ulma Kalthoum and the poet Cavafy.

▶**Cairo has been a place** of human settlement for thousands of years. It became the capital of the country in about A.D. 640, but during the tenth century the city became a center of Muslim learning. It is still home to important Islamic universities and mosques. The modern city is the biggest and most fascinating in Africa. Domes and minarets jostle with modern skyscrapers, and people from all over the continent live there.

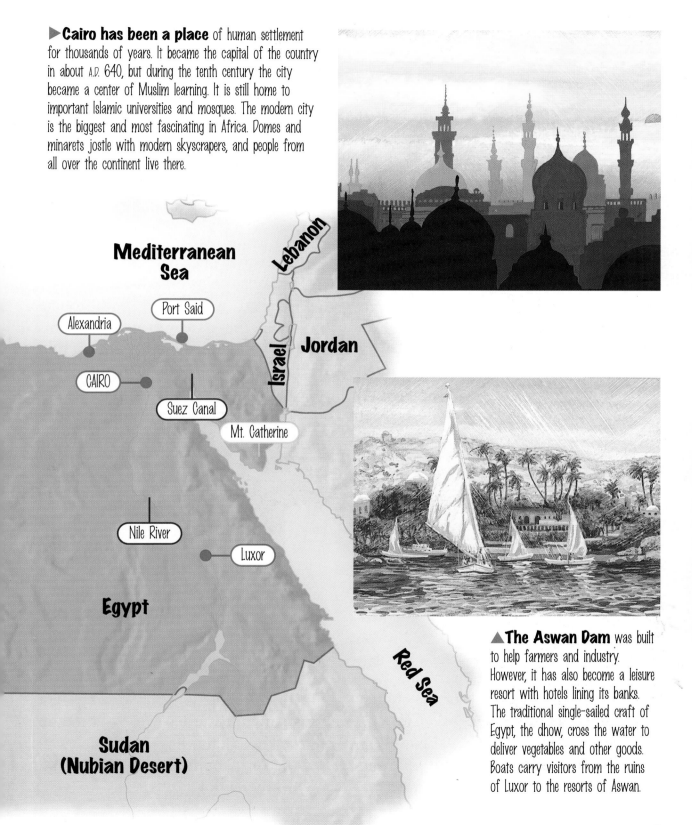

Mediterranean
Sea

Lebanon

Port Said

Alexandria

Israel   **Jordan**

CAIRO

Suez Canal

Mt. Catherine

Nile River

Luxor

Egypt

Red Sea

**Sudan
(Nubian Desert)**

▲**The Aswan Dam** was built to help farmers and industry. However, it has also become a leisure resort with hotels lining its banks. The traditional single-sailed craft of Egypt, the dhow, cross the water to deliver vegetables and other goods. Boats carry visitors from the ruins of Luxor to the resorts of Aswan.

RELIGIONS

Most Egyptians are Muslim. This means they follow the teachings of the prophet Mohammed. A small Christian community has been part of Egyptian life for nearly 2,000 years.

IN EGYPT nearly everybody is Muslim, but about one in ten people is a Coptic Christian. However, the Christian community in Egypt is one of the oldest in the world.

Egypt was part of the Roman Empire that ruled over large areas of both the Mediterranean coast and Europe. The empire collapsed in the fourth century A.D.

In the last 200 years of Roman rule there were a lot of Christians in Egypt. In the fifth century the Christians fell out with the head church in Constantinople, now known as Istanbul in Turkey. Since that time the Egyptian branch of the church has been known as the Coptic Church.

In the seventh century Egypt was conquered by the Arabs, who followed the ways of the prophet Mohammed.

Egypt became part of the Arab world that lay to its east. It was ruled by the Mamluks, who fell to the Ottoman Empire in the sixteenth century. This was a powerful Muslim government that ruled from Turkey. By this time the majority of Egyptians were part of the Muslim faith.

Over the centuries many mosques, most of them very beautiful, were built in Egypt. The world's oldest university, Al Azhar in Cairo, was founded to help Muslims study the Koran. This is the holy book of the Muslim faith.

The Coptic Church also built fine religious houses. The first Christian monasteries were started in Egypt. The church has a pope and still uses the old Coptic language although now everyone in Egypt speaks Arabic.

GREETINGS FROM **EGYPT!**

When the Arabs settled in Egypt more than 1,000 years ago, they brought their language with them. At the time the people were ruled from Rome and then Constantinople. Although Christianity flourished, Judaism, the faith of the Jewish people, and various local religions were also part of Egyptian life. The different groups spoke their own languages. Today, all Egyptians speak Arabic. There are at least 70 million Egyptians. Most of them live in the Nile valley, but some, called Bedouins, live in the desert. They are nomads who move around in search of pastures.

How do you say...

Hello
As-salaamu aleikum

How are you?
Izziak?

My name is ...
Ismi ...

Goodbye
Ma'a salaana

Thank you
Shukran

Peace
Salaam

MULID EN-NABI

The birthday of the prophet Mohammed is called the Mulid En-Nabi in Arabic. It is celebrated by all Muslims.

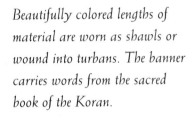

The birthday of the blessed prophet Mohammed falls on twelfth Rabei' el Awwal, which is the third Muslim month. Celebrations start from the beginning of the month. The eleventh day of the festival is called the Blessed Night, and in towns and little villages throughout the country, huge processions of pilgrims take place.

Different religious orders take part. They wear colorful turbans and headbands and also carry banners. *Dervishes*, who are communities of religious dancers, whirl about while crowds chant their praises to God. In the evening there are fireworks displays and recitals of religious songs. In Upper Egypt horse-races take place. These kick up clouds of dust in the dry desert sands.

Celebrations are also held at home.

Beautifully colored lengths of material are worn as shawls or wound into turbans. The banner carries words from the sacred book of the Koran.

THE MUSLIM YEAR

Muslims all over the world follow their own special calendar for religious events. They start their calendar from the time Mohammed moved from Mecca to the city of Medina. Christians start their calendar from the time of Christ.

The Muslim calendar is divided into months based on the phases of the moon. This means the months on the Muslim calendar are irregular. The beginning of each month is decided when the new moon of the next month is seen by specially chosen Muslim scholars. The calendar moves backward 11 days every year. A date that falls on July 20 this year will fall on July 9 next year.

Parents give their children sweets: sugar dolls for the girls and sugar horses for the boys. They also tell them stories from the *Hadith*, a life of Mohammed that was compiled by his followers soon after the prophet died.

Egyptian candies and cookies often use honey for sweetness and nuts for texture. At this festival the children are given special candy as a present, but there is a plentiful supply of other delicious foods, such as nut brittle and nougat.

AL-SAYIDA ZEINAB

This is one of the most popular festivals in Egypt, a time when millions of people come to Cairo for two weeks of music and celebration.

The festival of *Al-Sayida Zeinab* is one of the most popular in Egypt. It turns into a street party for as many as a quarter of a million people. Al-Sayida Zeinab, who was the granddaughter of the prophet Mohammed, is Cairo's patron saint, and one quarter in the city is named after her. Millions of people from all over Egypt come to Cairo to stay for two weeks and join in celebrating the

Street musicians are vital to the creation of the party atmosphere that takes hold of Cairo during the annual festival of Al-Sayida Zeinab. Musicians get together in bands and play on a variety of instruments.

10

memory of Al-Sayida Zeinab's visit to Cairo.

Families camp in the streets, bringing with them food, drink, mattresses, bedding, and gas stoves to cook on. Tents are set up by the different Sufi groups. There are fair rides and magic shows to entertain the children, and stalls sell party hats, sugar dolls, pancakes, and cotton candy.

At sunset bands start to play, and the dancing can go on all night. Usually, the instruments used are a drum called a *tabla*, an Egyptian violin, and a type of clarinet called a *mizmar*. In some instances the

Puffy pancakes, called fetir, are made in copper ovens on carts. The pancakes are made from flour and water, sprinkled with sugar, nuts, and raisins and then rolled up.

singer repeats God's name over and over.

Who are the Sufis? These are ordinary people who come

Dried fruits are common in Egypt and are added to many dishes, both sweet and savory. Dried apricots and prunes are the main ingredients used in this fruit salad.

together to worship God by working themselves into a trance by dancing and chanting the name of God. The whirling dervishes are Sufis. It is not known exactly how many Egyptians belong to Sufi orders.

ABU EL-HAGGAG

This is one of the biggest festivals in Egypt. The people dress up for evenings of horseracing, music, and visiting with friends.

The festival of *Abu El-Haggag* happens in the Muslim month of Sha'aban. The people of Luxor and the countryside around are in party mood as they gather to celebrate the life of their patron saint, Yussef Abu El-Haggag.

This holy man was born in the city of Damascus, in Syria, around A.D. 1150. He traveled to Egypt when he was in his fifties. While living there, El-Haggag set up a religious order, or group. Those who join his group are Sufis, people who believe whirling and dancing take them very close to spiritual knowledge.

The festival takes place in Luxor. In ancient times this was a big religious center, and the ruins of the old temple are still very much part of the modern town. Built among the

To Egyptians, turquoise is a healing symbol, and the scarab a symbol of wealth. These beliefs are very old, and turquoise scarabs and beads are sold at mulids.

wonderful ruins is a mosque that is dedicated to Abu El-Haggag. The mosque is precious to the local people who will not allow it to be moved out of the shelter of the old buildings.

Festivals held for holy people are called *mulids*. Crowds visit Luxor for the Mulid Sidi Abu El-Haggag because it is popular.

The festival ends with a big parade. Sufis, all representing their orders, lead the way to the mosque of Abu El-Haggag. They are followed closely by tradespeople on floats who show off their trade. For instance, carriage makers like to carry a big carriage through the streets of the town.

The focus of the parade falls on three model boats, which

At the festival perfume is sold in glass bottles that are copies of ones found in the ancient ruins. Simple bean dishes served with bread are on sale, too.

are carried on men's shoulders. People say that this tradition goes back to boat rituals found in the Ancient Egyptian religion. In Islam, however, boats symbolize a pilgrim's journey to Mecca.

Thousands collect around the mosque to listen to music or watch the horseraces. Sometimes the finish line seems to be where the crowd is!

13

PHARAOH'S BOAT

The ancient Egyptians had many festivals. One of the most important was to the Sun God Ra, who was said to travel across the sky in his boat every day.

IN THE BEGINNING there was nothing except a vast watery waste called the Waters of Chaos. One day something began to appear on the surface. It was a beautiful lotus flower. Gradually, the flower opened to reveal a golden child called Ra sitting within its petals.

Eventually, he grew lonely in his lotus surrounded only by the dark waters and the serpents of chaos that tried to kill him. One day, while looking out across the expanse of water, he decided he needed some company. So he created the other gods, the sky, the earth, and human beings.

He made the River Nile and its fertile valley for his people and protected them with vast expanses of desert. Last of all, he made the Beautiful West, where everyone, gods and humans, could go when they died. When Ra had created Order, he was very pleased. At last he had company, but he could not get rid of the Waters of Chaos.

For many centuries he ruled over the land of Egypt wisely and justly. Everyone was happy, and his children, the lesser gods, thrived.

Each day Ra traveled through his dominions on his vessel, the Boat of a Million Years, bringing

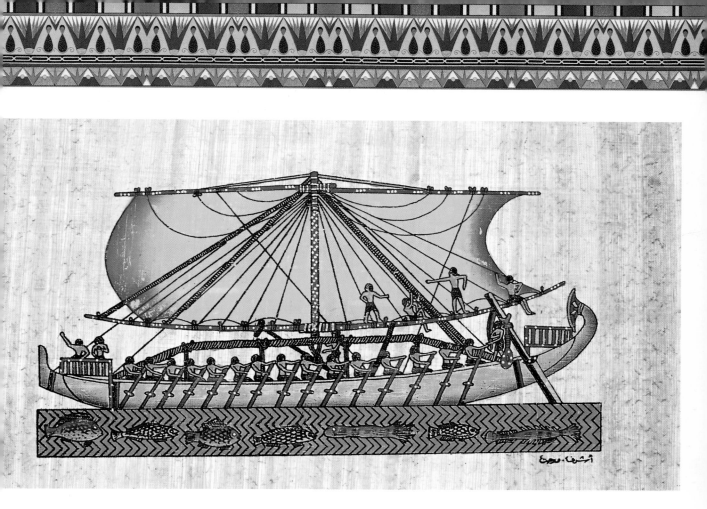

with him the sunlight. But every
night he was forced to board the
Night Boat and travel through the
Waters of Chaos, which still
surged beneath the earth and the
underworld. During this time the
world was left in darkness

His children traveled with
him. Thoth, the god of wisdom,
gave him advice. Hathor, who was
the goddess of love, protected him
with her benevolence, and Seth,
his strongest son, fought off the
evil serpents of Chaos that tried to
kill Ra and bring darkness to his
dominions forever.

Every day was a battle
between Order and Chaos. In
order for the new day to dawn, Ra
had to make the perilous journey
through Chaos with the help of
the other gods.

HOW TO MAKE YOUR OWN PAPER

The ancient Egyptians used a water plant called papyrus to make paper. Make your own colored paper by recycling old sheets of white paper and dyeing them with colored inks.

Papyrus was cultivated on the banks of the River Nile by the ancient Egyptians. The stems were used to make cloth, sails, and mats, but its most important use was for making paper. This paper was used for legal documents, for writing letters, and to make books in the form of scrolls.

YOU WILL NEED

An old picture frame
A stocking
Large needle; thick cotton
Sheets of white paper
A bucket
A large plastic bowl
Pieces of straw
Colored inks
Pieces of cloth
Old newspaper

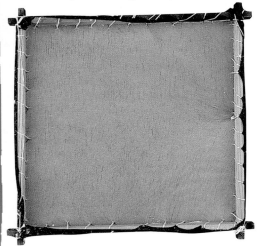

2 Tear up the white paper into small pieces and soak the pieces overnight in a bucket of warm water. Stir and squeeze the mixture from time to time with your hands. You can speed this up by putting the paper in a food processor.

1 Take the old picture frame. Cut a square the size of the frame out of the stocking. Stretch the square of stocking and sew it to the frame. This paper-making frame is called a deckle.

3 Put the mixture into a large bowl and add enough water to make a very watery pulp. You can add bits of chopped-up straw and drops of colored ink at this stage. Dip the deckle into the pulp and bring it up. Let some of the water drip through.

4 Turn the deckle over. Place it pulp side down onto a piece of cloth under which is a pile of newspaper. Press down on the deckle to squeeze out the water. Slowly lift the deckle, leaving behind paper pulp. Lay another piece of cloth on paper pulp and repeat process. When you have a pile of paper, press down on it to squeeze out more water, then carefully separate the pieces. Lay flat to dry.

RAMADAN

Ramadan *is the Muslim month of fasting. It commemorates the time when the Koran and the religion of Islam were revealed by God to the prophet Mohammed.*

The ninth month in the Hijra calendar is called *Ramadan*. During this month good Muslims will try not to drink, eat, or smoke in the daytime. This can be very difficult when Ramadan falls in the summer months and temperatures go up to 104°F. This is why an exception is made for the sick or elderly, small children, and pregnant women.

People break their fast by eating a date or drinking water bought from water bearers. The picture below shows typical food eaten at the end of Ramadan.

Each day of the fast begins before dawn when the family has the nighttime meal called *Sahur.* This meal usually consists of white cheese and yogurt, and a bean and olive oil dish called *ful mudames.*

When the sun sets, the feasting begins. The evening meal is called *Iftar.* Wealthy people put tables of food in the street for the poor. At night, after Iftar, people walk in the streets. Children are allowed to stay up late during Ramadan.

On the last day people gather at home to watch television, or they go to mosques to wait to hear the announcement of the rising of the new moon. This signals the end of Ramadan. Then it's time to begin the three-day party that is called *Eid Al-Fitr*.

Everyone goes to the mosques or local shrines at Eid Al-Fitr, but before they go out to pray, Muslims must give some money to someone they know is poor. This money is called the *Zakat Al-Fitr*.

Hot, sweet mint tea is popular in the evenings during Ramadan but is drunk throughout the year. In restaurants the sugar is already added, and the sweetness of the tea is varied according to how many times it is stirred — from once for sweet, to four for very sweet.

MUSLIM HOLIDAYS

All Muslim holidays begin at sunset. So they seem to start the day before you might expect. Nowadays special calendars are published to show Egyptians exactly what times festivals start. Traditionally, to decide when a new day had dawned, a holy man went to the top of the minaret, the tall spire on a mosque, and held up a black thread and a white thread. When he could tell the two apart, the new day had officially begun.

During Ramadan the fast should only be broken when it is announced from the loudspeakers on minarets. At the same time the colored lights that decorate the mosques during Ramadan are switched on.

MAKE A SHADOOF

The shadoof has been used in Egypt since ancient times to irrigate the land. It even appears in ancient Egyptian tomb paintings. Make a model shadoof using sticks, clay, and raffia. You can add a clay model of a farmer using the shadoof.

The River Nile running through Egypt is the longest river in the world. Every year it floods, making the soil in the Nile valley very fertile. To help grow crops, this soil is irrigated with water from the Nile. The shadoof is used to transfer the water from the river into irrigation channels. This method has been effective for thousands of years and is still used today.

YOU WILL NEED
Air-hardening clay
A ball of raffia
3 wooden sticks 12" long
All-purpose glue
4 lengths of raffia 16" long
1 wooden stick 16" long

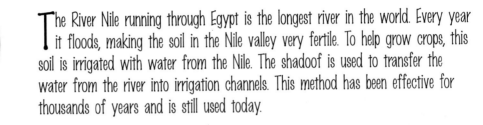

1 Mold a bucket and a rock from air-hardening clay. Make two holes through the top of the bucket. Take the ball of raffia and cut two strands. Thread the strands through the holes in the bucket and then tie the strands together to make a handle for the bucket.

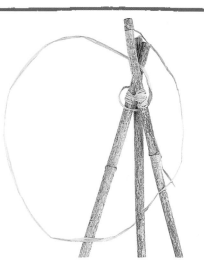

3 Take four pieces of 16" raffia and tie them together at their middles (A) to make eight strands. Put these into pairs and, 1" from center knot (A) tie the pairs together (B). Separate the pairs and make new pairs by joining each strand with one from an adjacent knot. Tie these together (C). These knots must be 1" from knots (B). You now have a net to hold the clay stone.

2 Take three 12" sticks and tie them together at the top. Spread the ends of the sticks to make a tripod. Put some glue 1" from the bottom of the sticks. Wrap raffia around glue of one leg, stretch raffia to next leg and repeat until raffia stretches between three legs.

4 Place clay rock into raffia net. Tie loose ends of net around the top of the rock. Take 16" stick and tie the bucket 1" from one end. Tie the rock and basket 1" from the opposite end. Balance the stick on your tripod. You now have a shadoof.

21

EID AL-ADHA

*The last month of the Islamic Year is an exciting one for Egyptians. It is the month of the "Big Feast," or **Eid Al-Adha,** and of the pilgrimage to Mecca.*

Eid Al-Adha takes place on the tenth day of the month of *Dhul-Hijja*. This is the Feast of the Sacrifice, the time when every family that can afford to do so slaughters a sheep. For at least a week beforehand the animal will have been given a lot to eat. In cities people keep them on the roof to keep them safe. Early in the morning, after Eid prayer, the animal is slaughtered quickly in the *Halal* way, which means the blood is drained from the body. In villages, to bring good luck, the children may dip their hands in the blood and then make handprints on the walls outside their houses.

This feast is held to commemorate the time the prophet Abraham was going to sacrifice his son Isaac because he believed it to be the will of God. It reminds Muslims that they must submit to the will of Allah, that is, God.

THE FIVE PILLARS OF ISLAM

Good Muslims must be decent and honest, but to guarantee a place in paradise, they must:

1. Believe in one God and that Mohammed is his prophet
2. Pray, facing Mecca, five times a day
3. Give alms to the poor
4. Fast during the month of Ramadan
5. Go to Mecca once in a lifetime.

Ramadan is Come!
Ramadan, Ramadan,
Ramadan is come.
The sultan's daughter, ee yo ha.
In a kaftan garbed, ee yo ha.
Ramadan, Ramadan,
Ramadan is come.

This decorative wall hanging shows Mecca, the birthplace of Mohammed. During the month of Dhul-Hijja many Muslims make the pilgrimage to Mecca.

WAHAWI YA WAHAWI

Wa - ha - wi ya wa - ha - wi ee yo——— ha.

Bin - till—— Sul - tan ee yo——— ha.

Lab - sa—— kof - tan ee yo——— ha.

Wa - ha - wi ya wa - ha - wi ee yo——— ha.

SHAM EN NESSEEM

Ever since the times of the pharaohs Egyptians have celebrated the arrival of spring with **Sham En Nesseem,** *which means "Sniff the Breeze."*

The festival of *Sham En Nesseem* falls according to the Christian calendar rather than to the Muslim calendar, so it always comes soon after Easter. The day is a national holiday, and both Muslims and Christians alike take the opportunity to spend the day out of doors and enjoy the natural world.

The coming of the new season has been celebrated in various ways in Egypt for thousands of years. In a country where farming is so important, the arrival of spring, with all its promise of new crops, is a time to be marked by celebration.

Everyone puts on new clothes specially for the occasion and then goes out for a picnic. While some families may choose to sit by the

The Coptic cross is the symbol of the Egyptian Christians. Street vendors are a familiar sight during festivals. Business is particularly brisk for those who sell food.

CHICK PEAS AND SPINACH

Rinse the chick peas, drain them, and put them in a pan. Thoroughly rinse the spinach, shake off any excess water, and roughly chop it. Add the spinach to the chick peas in the pan. Cook, stirring over a medium heat until the chick peas are hot and the spinach is soft. Season with the pepper. Remove the pan from the heat and set to one side.

In another pan heat the oil. Add the garlic and coriander. Fry just long enough for the garlic to become soft — do not allow it to burn. Pour the oil, garlic, and coriander over the chick peas and spinach. Stir to mix well. Heat the ingredients through and serve.

SERVES SIX
1 15-oz. can chick peas
2 lb. fresh spinach
$\frac{1}{2}$ t. pepper
4 T. olive oil
3 cloves garlic, peeled and chopped
1 t. ground coriander

waters of the Nile, others may go to visit the family graves instead.

In the villages you can see farming folk setting off in the morning on freshly painted donkey carts. Sometimes even the donkeys get to wear a new set of beads for the spring. The beads are made of turquoise, which is said to ward off the evil eye, or evil thoughts of others.

In cities the parks are thronged with huge family gatherings. Everyone, from elderly grandparents to tiny tots, gets together to enjoy the good weather.

The picnic may be simple or elaborate, but it always has to include salt fish and onion. These foods are said to stop disease. Colored eggs are also eaten. They are an important symbol of new life.

Boiled eggs with colored shells are usually included in the Sham En Nesseem picnic. To Muslims and Christians alike, eggs represent birth and the new life of spring.

25

SAINT GEORGE

*Saint George is the patron saint of Egyptian Christians, who call him **Mari Girgis**. In Cairo a festival is held on April 23 in his honor.*

MANY YEARS AGO, in about the fourth century, an evil dragon was spreading fear throughout the countryside. All the people were afraid of the flames it breathed from its terrible jaws. Every day it came, breathing and hissing fire, to demand food. It was never satisfied until it had devoured two whole sheep. Eventually, the people of the area ran out of sheep and did not know what to do. The dragon demanded human flesh instead.

The people realized they had no choice. Their king decided that the only way to choose who would be fed to the dragon was by drawing lots. Everyone's name was put on a piece of paper and put into a basket. The king regularly took out one of the names. The person whose name was pulled out was tied to a tree to await their death in the dragon's jaws.

One day the name of the king's daughter, a beautiful girl with flowing hair, was chosen from the basket. The king demanded that lots be drawn again. He told his daughter that because she was a princess, she could be spared the fiery jaws of the dragon. She was brave, however, and told him that she must go to her fate for the good of her people. She dressed in the white

bridal robe that she would never wear to her own wedding and was tied to a tree to await the dragon.

George heard of the princess's cruel destiny and determined to rescue her. The dragon was advancing upon the princess when George arrived on his white horse. The beast hissed and spat fire, but George was not afraid. With his lance he pierced the dragon's mouth. The beast twisted and writhed as it struggled to free itself, but Saint George was stronger. He cut the ropes that tied the princess and, taking her girdle, he twisted it tightly around the scaly neck of the dragon. He dragged the beast to the king, declaring that he would kill it if his subjects would become Christians. Fifteen thousand people converted immediately, and the dragon was killed.

COPTIC CHRISTMAS

Like all Orthodox Christians from the Middle East and Russia, Egyptian Copts celebrate Christmas on January 7.

Icons are religious paintings that are venerated in Coptic churches. This means that they are treated with special respect and awe.

Finger cymbals are often used in the folk music of Egypt. They are small and portable, which makes them perfect for family use.

The Copts spend a large part of the year fasting. Like many other Christians, the faithful abstain from meat and dairy products during Lent, the 40 days before Easter. But unusually, they do the same for the 43 days leading up to Christmas.

Members of the Coptic Church are asked to fast at regular times throughout the year. These fasts generally follow the suffering of a biblical figure. The Christmas fast recalls the fasting of the prophet Moses. After he had fasted, God gave him the Ten Commandments written on tablets of stone.

On Christmas Eve everyone in the family is given a new suit of clothes. These are worn to go to the Midnight Mass. In Cairo the Coptic pope himself gives the sermon. The churches are decorated and lit with lamps and tall candles. After Mass everyone goes home to a meal of turkey.

On Christmas Day people either visit relatives and friends or entertain at home. Guests bring biscuits, which are similar to shortbread, to share. The hosts provide soft drinks.

At Christmas Copts give lamps and candles as gifts. They believe Joseph, Mary's husband, lit lamps to light the stable in Bethlehem during the birth of Jesus Christ 2,000 years ago.

This is a copy of a Byzantine cross. The eastern churches of the Byzantine Empire, such as the Coptic Church, separated from the Catholic Church in the fifth century A.D.

CHRISTMAS COOKIES

MAKES 12 TO 16

2 oz. unsalted butter
2 t. sugar
1 egg yolk
2 cups flour
caster sugar
silver balls

Preheat the oven to 380°F. Grease a baking sheet and set to one side. Beat the butter and the sugar together until pale and fluffy. Beat the egg yolk. Add this to the butter and sugar mixture and beat lightly until smooth. Add the flour and stir in to make a stiff dough.

Cut the dough into equal pieces and use your hands to shape them into small balls. Decorate half the cookies with the caster sugar and the other half with the silver balls. Place them on a greased baking sheet. Bake for 10 to 15 minutes, or until the cookies are a golden color. Leave them to cool and then serve.

COPTIC EASTER

Christians believe that during Easter Christ was put to death and that three days later He came back to life, or was resurrected. Easter is a celebration of Christ's resurrection.

Easter is the most important festival for Egyptian Christians. Easter week begins with Palm Sunday, when a special midnight service is held in remembrance of Jesus's entry into Jerusalem. Here He was greeted by people laying palm leaves in front of Him.

The climax of Easter week is on Saturday night when Christians go to church. The service is long and goes on well after midnight. At the end of the service the priests walk through the candle-lit church, where they swing incense burners and bless the congregation. On the night of the resurrection people break a 55-day-long fast, sometimes with a stuffed leg of lamb.

WORDS TO KNOW

Coptic Church: The Christian Church in Egypt

Dancing dervish: A Muslim who has taken vows of poverty and shows his or her faith through dance.

Fast: To go without some or all kinds of food and drink deliberately.

Halal: Meat that has been prepared according to Muslim law.

Koran: The Islamic holy book, believed to be the word of God as told to the prophet Mohammed.

Lent: The 40 days between Ash Wednesday and Easter.

Mecca: The birthplace of Mohammed. Mecca is the most important place of pilgrimage for Muslims.

Minaret: The tall tower of a mosque from which Muslims are called to prayer.

Mosque: A place of worship for Muslims.

Muslim: A follower of the religion of Islam.

Nomads: People who travel all or some of the time in search of food for their animals.

Papyrus: A water plant used to make paper in Ancient Egypt.

Patron saint: A saint who is special to a particular group. Nations, towns, and professions all have patron saints.

Pilgrim: A person who makes a religious journey, or pilgrimage, to a holy place.

Prophet: A teacher or interpreter of the will of God.

Ramadan: The ninth month of the Muslim year, during which Muslims fast from dawn until sunset.

Sacrifice: To give up something that is greatly valued for an even more important reason.

Shrine: A place that is sacred to the memory of a holy person.

Sufi: A Muslim holy man.

ACKNOWLEDGMENTS

WITH THANKS TO:
Lorin Watt, Oxford.
Articles of Faith.

PHOTOGRAPHY:
All photographs by Bruce Mackie except: John Elliott p. 25. Marshall Cavendish pp. 13, 18. Cover photograph by Corbis/Owen Franken.

ILLUSTRATIONS BY:
Fiona Saunders pp. 4 – 5. Tracy Rich p. 7.
Maps by John Woolford.

Recipes: Ellen Dupont.

Set Contents